W9-CNA-834

Recycling

Look for these and other books in the Lucent
Overview series:

Abortion
Acid Rain
AIDS
Alcoholism
Animal Rights
The Beginning of Writing
Cancer
Dealing with Death
Death Penalty
Drugs and Sports
Drug Trafficking
Eating Disorders
Endangered Species
Energy Alternatives
Extraterrestrial Life
Gangs
Garbage
Greenhouse Effect
Gun Control
Hazardous Waste
The Holocaust
Homeless Children
Ocean Pollution
Oil Spills
The Olympic Games
Ozone
Population
Rainforests
Recycling
Smoking
Special Effects in the Movies
Teen Alcoholism
Teen Pregnancy
The UFO Challenge
Vietnam

Recycling

by Don Nardo

LUCENT
B·O·O·K·S

LUCENT Overview Series

OUR ENDANGERED PLANET

LUCENT *Overview Series* ⎯ OUR ENDANGERED PLANET

Library of Congress Cataloging-in-Publication Data

Nardo, Don, 1947-
    Recycling / by Don Nardo.
        p.   cm. — (Lucent overview series)
    Includes bibliographical references and index.
    Summary: Discusses recycling, its value and realities, and the search for
innovative recycling ideas.
    ISBN 1-56006-135-9 (acid-free)
    1. Recycling (Waste, etc.)—Juvenile literature.   [1. Recycling (Waste)]
I. Title.   II. Series.
TD794.5.N35   1992
363.72'82—dc20
                                                    92-27849
                                                       CIP
                                                        AC

© Copyright 1992 by Lucent Books, Inc.
P.O. Box 289011, San Diego, CA 92198-9011

Contents

CHAPTER ONE   7
Recycling: A Valuable and Necessary Process

CHAPTER TWO   17
An Old Idea Comes of Age

CHAPTER THREE   31
Recycling and the Environment

CHAPTER FOUR   49
Recycling Realities

CHAPTER FIVE   65
Searching for Innovative Ideas

APPENDIX   80
Three Recycling Programs

ORGANIZATIONS TO CONTACT   86
SUGGESTIONS FOR FURTHER READING   89
WORKS CONSULTED   90
INDEX   92
ABOUT THE AUTHOR   95
PICTURE CREDITS   96

1

Recycling: A Valuable and Necessary Process

AT THE END of each week, Cathy Tallen, a nurse and homemaker living in Colrain, Massachusetts, collects her daily newspapers, stacks and ties them, and drops them off at a paper collection center on her way to work. In Brunswick, Maine, homeowners Arleen and Roger Rancourt regularly collect their empty aluminum soft drink cans. Twice a month they take them to a local redemption center where they receive five cents for each can turned in. Representatives of the Amoco Chemical company travel from town to town in New York State urging workers at school cafeterias and restaurants to save their discarded polystyrene foam containers. Amoco sponsors a special program designed to collect large quantities of these containers, which would otherwise end up in trash bins.

All of these people, along with millions of others around the United States, demonstrate an awareness of and responsibility for what happens to the things they throw away. They all routinely recycle portions of their refuse. Recycling is the process of collecting discarded items of garbage

(Opposite page) Workers at an aluminum recycling plant send compacted bales of aluminum cans up a conveyor to be processed into reusable aluminum.

A family watches as the aluminum cans they have brought to the recycling center begin the recycling process.

or trash and reusing them in some constructive way. Sometimes people simply reuse the items for the same purpose. For example, the glass soda bottles collected in Maine and many other states are sent back to soft drink plants, sterilized, and refilled. Another way people recycle wastes is by making new products from the materials the wastes are composed of. The foam containers collected by Amoco, for instance, undergo a process that crushes them and mixes them with chemicals. The result is a new material used to make housing insulation boards, cafeteria trays, and various office products. Old newspapers also undergo a physical and chemical transformation process. Industries then use the material created to make either more newspapers or a host of other paper products. All over the country and in many other parts of the world, individuals, communities, and companies regularly recycle millions of discarded items and materials. And the recycling industry is constantly expanding.

Why people recycle

The reason that so many people and organizations in the United States are recycling is that they are concerned about the country's increasingly serious environmental problems. One of these problems is the rapid depletion of natural resources for use in industry and manufacturing. People are using up such vital commodities as oil, trees, and metals at increasing rates. Because only a limited amount of these resources exists in nature, there is a real danger that they might eventually be used up entirely. In addition, the methods used to collect and process these resources often pollute the environment. For example, the regular drilling and transporting of oil results in more than ten thousand oil spills yearly worldwide. And the process of making plastics from oil releases toxic gases into the atmosphere. Recycling helps alleviate these problems. When people recycle plastics, less oil has to be drilled, helping conserve an important natural resource. At the same time, fewer plastic products need to be manufactured, reducing the amount of air pollution. Recycling products made from trees and various metals similarly helps conserve resources and reduce environmental pollution.

Refuse disposal is another serious environmental concern in the United States. An examination of the huge scope of the refuse problem shows why recycling has become increasingly important and popular in recent years. Americans produce a

Workers from the environmentalist organization Greenpeace clean up sludge from a paper-processing plant that pollutes a nearby stream.

depletion -
① to empty as the body
unload as the
vessels of the
by purgation,
② To exhaust, as of
strength

tremendous amount of garbage and trash. This is partly because they buy and use so many products. When these products are used up, they or the containers they come in become refuse or trash. Because the population of the country increases each year, the volume of products bought and, therefore, the amount of refuse produced also increase. Says Gary Branson in his book *Recycling at Home*:

> Consider the population growth, then consider that each of us contributes about 3½ pounds of waste to the pile *each day*, for a total generation of about 1,200 pounds of waste per person, per year. Unless we take control of the situation it will certainly get worse: each decade several thousand new products appear on supermarket shelves. There are spraycans filled with chemicals we didn't know we needed, disposable diapers, electrical gadgets, and single-item packaging, to name but a few recent arrivals.

Whether packaging contains a single item or several, it contributes enormously to the refuse problem. Practically everything bought in stores today comes in some kind of packaging—usually paper, cardboard, or plastic. Throwing away that packaging generates millions of tons of refuse each year.

A throwaway society

The thousands of products designed for quick use and disposal include newspapers, ballpoint pens, portable lighters, paint cans, juice and egg cartons, mailing envelopes, magazines, and lottery tickets. Each year, Americans throw away 2 billion disposable razors, 18 billion disposable diapers, 30 billion tin cans, 220 million tires, 2.6 billion batteries, 25 billion Styrofoam cups, and 35 billion tons of yard waste. People in the United States also discard some 67 million tons of paper each year. American offices alone throw away enough paper yearly to build a twelve-foot-high

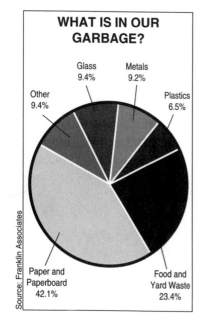

WHAT IS IN OUR GARBAGE?

Glass 9.4%
Metals 9.2%
Other 9.4%
Plastics 6.5%
Paper and Paperboard 42.1%
Food and Yard Waste 23.4%

Source: Franklin Associates

wall stretching from Los Angeles to New York.

The total amount of solid wastes generated yearly by U.S. consumers in their homes and workplaces is a staggering 420 million tons. That is enough refuse to fill up 5.8 million large trailer trucks. Stacked one on top of the other, these trucks would create a tower of trash more than 16,300 miles high! And this does not include the waste materials generated by industry, agriculture, and mining, which are at least ten times more than the consumer-generated refuse. Altogether, the United States produces more than 4 billion tons of trash and garbage each year. A stack of trucks carrying this mass would stretch more than halfway to the moon. It is no wonder

This pile of trash is just a drop in the ocean of garbage produced every day in America. Recycling is one part of the solution to the problem of America's garbage glut.

that many people refer to the United States as a throwaway society.

But the United States is not the only throwaway society in the world. Indeed, reports John E. Young in the magazine *World Watch*:

> Mounting piles of garbage are a feature of virtually all industrial market nations. In the Organization for Economic Cooperation and Development (OECD)—the consortium [association] of industrial countries—14 of the 16 members . . . showed increases in solid waste generation per person between 1980 and 1985, and garbage production now appears to be on the rise in Japan and . . . Germany.

Japan, with more than 125 million people living in a land area slightly smaller than the state of California, has serious refuse problems. In 1975 the city of Hiroshima found that it could no longer cope with its mounting piles of garbage and declared a "garbage emergency." Through large-scale recycling and other methods, the city learned to manage its refuse. But most other Japanese cities have not done so well, and in the early 1990s the country faces a potential garbage crisis. Many other nations find themselves in similar predicaments. Ireland, Spain, Canada, Norway, Britain, and Switzerland are just some of the countries that reported large increases in trash generation between 1980 and 1992.

Burning and burying refuse

Why have so many countries allowed their refuse problems to become so serious? The answer lies mainly in the relative newness of the problem. The worldwide garbage dilemma is largely a by-product of the modern industrial age, especially the twentieth century. Before products were produced and packaged on a mass scale, refuse problems in most societies were minimal. The standard methods for dealing with trash were burning it and burying it. The Romans and most other ancient and medieval peoples used these methods, and people around the world still routinely burned and buried their garbage in the early 1900s. Few people then foresaw that the volume of garbage would increase so sharply in the mid-twentieth century. And when it did, most towns, states, and countries continued to use the solutions that had worked in the past.

But eventually it became evident that the old ways of dealing with garbage had drawbacks when used on a massive scale. Burning, officially called incineration, pours smoke, ash, and often toxic pollutants into the atmosphere. In large

Incinerators can reduce the volume of today's garbage to some extent, but heaps of ash remain.

amounts, these pollutants can be harmful to plants, animals, and people. Another drawback of burning garbage is that large, modern incinerators are expensive to build and operate.

Burying garbage in dumps known as landfills also has its drawbacks when dealing with trash on a huge scale. The most pressing problem is finding enough space for the trash. As the volume of refuse rose sharply in the second half of the twentieth century, existing landfills in the United States quickly filled up. Towns often expanded them but even the larger ones had trouble keeping up with the wastes generated by rapidly growing populations. So, by the early 1980s many landfills in the country were running out of space and closing. According to the U.S. Environmental Protection Agency, or EPA, the United States had some

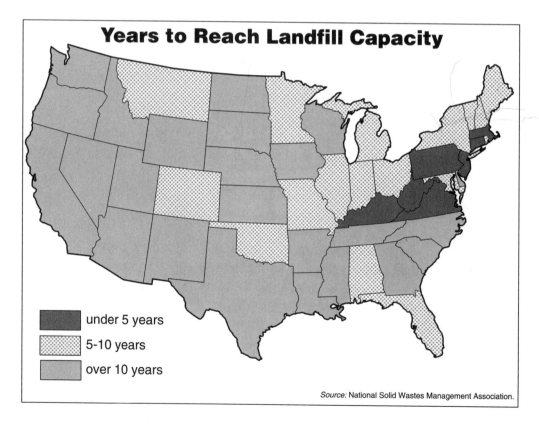

Years to Reach Landfill Capacity

under 5 years
5-10 years
over 10 years

Source: National Solid Wastes Management Association.

twenty thousand landfills in 1978. That number had dropped below seven thousand by 1988.

While the number of landfills has drastically decreased, the flow of refuse continues to grow and the remaining landfills are straining to meet the need. According to Allen Blakey of the National Solid Wastes Management Association, a group that promotes solutions to the refuse problem, in 1992 ten states had less than five years of landfill capacity left. Many cities have serious landfill problems. Chicago will run out of space in its landfills by 1994. And Los Angeles faces the prospect of closing its landfills by 1995. This is not surprising considering that each year about 14 million tons of trash flow onto Los Angeles-area landfills, enough to fill Dodger Stadium every nine days! Virtually no new landfills are opening in the United States because nearly everywhere, owners of homes and businesses have made it clear that they do not want garbage dumps in their backyards.

Barges piled with garbage from New York City are towed out to sea. Many landfills in New York are full and the city is desperate to solve its burgeoning waste problem.

Alternate disposal methods needed

While incineration and landfills have their share of problems, few scientists and community leaders advocate eliminating these methods of trash disposal altogether. Both, when used carefully and on a moderate scale, are effective and relatively safe. But many people have come to realize that these methods alone are no longer enough. Alternate methods of dealing with refuse are needed.

Recycling has proven to be an important supplement to the standard refuse-disposal methods. The concept is simple and straightforward. The more materials that are recycled, the fewer are left to burn or bury. In a world swept by growing tidal waves of garbage, recycling has become an increasingly necessary and valuable process.

2

An Old Idea Comes of Age

WIDESPREAD PUBLIC INTEREST and participation in recycling began in the early 1970s, so it might appear that recycling is a relatively new idea. Yet recycling is actually an old idea used in various ways and at various times throughout the ages.

How recycling came about

Recycling as an organized activity began in the United States in the late 1700s. Traveling peddlers from towns in early New England states like New Hampshire and Massachusetts traded in junk and discarded scrap materials. As Charles Lipsett explains in his fascinating history of recycling:

(Opposite page) A junk collector tosses a bundle of old newspapers onto his cart in 1941 in New York. Americans were forced to recycle paper, metal, cloth, and other materials when the United States entered World War II.

> Years ago Boston, originally, was the center of U.S. commerce, and with New Hampshire became, practically, the birthplace of the Yankee tincart peddler. As the eighteenth century drew to a close, we saw young men from every established New England settlement taking to country roads, either on foot with packs on their backs, or on horseback with saddle-bags full of merchandise. Successful in their operations they became the owner of a horse and tincart—exchanging tinware [pots and pans] for rags and skins or pieces of copper or lead.

17

The peddlers sold their collected scrap to metal workers and other small manufacturers, who used it to make new products. In this way, the practice of recycling helped support the early beginnings of industry in the United States. One of the many people who built successful companies with the aid of the recycling trade was Abel Porter. Recounts Charles Lipsett:

Abel Porter and his brother arrived in Waterbury, Connecticut in the 1780s and joined forces with the Grilly Brothers, who had been making pewter [a mixture of tin and other metals] buttons from scrap. . . . The new organization took the name of Abel Porter and Company. . . . They set up a plant in Waterbury to produce brass [a mixture of copper and zinc] . . . obtaining their copper from scrap. They arranged with peddlers to pick up old

A drawing of a nineteenth-century rag collector pulling his jangling cart along a city street. Townspeople would give him rags, old clothes, and bits of metal. He would sell these to tradespeople to make into a variety of useful items.

copper objects, giving the peddler a different item to be used in exchange. . . . The newly made brass was cast in ingots and these were rolled into sheets in the rollers of a tiny iron mill in Litchfield [Connecticut].

Another early American businessman who encouraged and profited from recycling was the legendary Paul Revere. He bought old scrap metals from peddlers and also collected old silver coins. These he melted down and molded into new metal cups, bowls, and other items. Revere also founded the first copper mill in the United States on his farm in Canton, Massachusetts, in 1800. The copper he produced there from recycled metals became the copper sheathing for the Massachusetts statehouse dome and the bottom hull of the famous battleship *Constitution*.

The battleship Constitution, *one of the most famous warships in American history, had an outer hull made from metal recycled by Revolutionary War hero Paul Revere.*

Industry leads the way

During the 1800s, as the country expanded, scrap peddlers carried their recycling trade westward, exchanging goods with the pioneers and supporting the growth of new industries. Early factory owners around the country found it cheaper to buy old scrap metals than to mine and smelt metal ores. In order to save money, they regularly supplemented their mined metals with recycled ones. Thus, as in early New England, the recycling of various metals and other materials became a routine and vital industrial process in other sections of the country. In the same century, recycling also became a regular component of industry in other prosperous countries like Britain and France.

At no time was the importance of recycling to industry more evident than during the major wars of the twentieth century. Governments needed large amounts of metal to build ships, planes, tanks, guns, and other war materials. So the military organizations in each industrialized nation instituted massive recycling operations designed to collect as much scrap metal as possible.

In the United States during World War II, for instance, towns across the country set up scrap metal collection drives. At that time the government estimated there were some 6 million farms in the United States, each of which had up to five hundred pounds of scrap metal lying around. The U.S. Department of Agriculture sent out thousands of letters a day requesting farmers to turn in their scrap for recycling. Automobile junkyards became another prime source of recyclable metals. In the second half of 1942, for example, 450,000 junked cars flowed from junkyards to metal-recycling plants each month. Industry also recycled massive amounts of rubber and paper for the war effort. Industrial recycling became absolutely vital in wartime, says Charles Lipsett. The United States, he says, could not have won World War I and World War II without the scrap and waste materials recycled by industry.

Home recycling

Although most of the early recycling in the United States was industry- or war-related, some thrifty individuals engaged in small-scale recycling in their own homes. In the late 1800s, many housewives routinely saved empty oatmeal boxes and coffee cans, and turned them into containers for pencils, nails, yarn, and thousands of other items. Other common items recycled or reused at home were rags, string, tinfoil, and paper bags. However, most people who recycled this way did so mainly to help make ends meet. They did not recycle to help with the problems of refuse disposal, resource conservation, or saving the environment, since these had not yet become major public issues. So home recycling remained rela-

A bale of waste paper awaits delivery to a recycling plant during World War II. Some historians claim that the United States could not have won the two world wars without the recycling efforts of American industry.

tively infrequent and small in scale for many years.

Home recycling on a larger scale began in the 1970s. At that time the general public started to recognize that regular recycling by everyday citizens could aid resource conservation and the environment. The first Earth Day, a major media event, called attention to such environmental issues. It was staged in April 1970 in many cities and towns across the country by thousands of people concerned with the deteriorating condition

Students from a Butte, Montana, elementary school pose atop a heap of scrap metal they collected for recycling during World War II.

of the environment. Through rallies, meetings, speeches, and printed materials, ecologists and other experts stressed that people were using up natural resources too fast, discarding massive amounts of refuse, and polluting the environment in the process. Part of the proposed solution to these problems was the routine recycling of metals, glass, paper, and other materials in homes, schools, and offices.

At that time, M.J. Mighdoll, executive vice president of the National Association of Sec-

A group of citizens joins in a rally to promote saving the environment. In the 1970s, environmentalism, rather than economics, became the primary motivation for recycling by ordinary citizens.

ondary Material Industries, a group that promoted the reuse of scrap materials, summed up the new realization of the importance of recycling:

> Either we continue on the same self-defeating, downhill road we have been traveling, a road filled with dumps, landfills, smoking incinerators, litter—or we can take a new, hard look at these solid wastes. We can see them for what they are: potential new resources, waiting to be recycled and put to productive use for our society.

Annual celebrations of Earth Day followed. Thanks to these events and increased media attention to environmental problems, the idea of recycling quickly became popular with the public. Individuals, groups, and businesses across the country joined the effort. The Boy Scouts and Girl Scouts began holding regular drives to recycle glass, aluminum cans, and paper. Many towns and businesses set up collection centers for these scrap materials. Lola Redford, wife of actor Robert Redford, printed a newspaper to inform consumers about the benefits of recycling. The newspaper was printed on recycled paper. New York City and many other cities began requiring that a significant amount of the paper used in local government offices be made from recycled paper. AT&T set, and met, a goal of printing 50 percent of its telephone books on recycled paper by 1974.

Recycling becomes popular

At a hearing in June 1971, the U.S. Congress heard testimony from experts about recycling's economic potential for the country. This was the first time U.S. lawmakers publicly recognized the importance of recycling by individual consumers and communities. *Recycling* became such a popular catchword that many companies already in the scrap business changed their names to conform with the trend. Thus, in 1974 the National Association of Secondary Material Industries became the National Association of Recycling Industries.

Another aspect of recycling's new popularity was the rise of the so-called Green Movement. This was the marketing of products labeled "recycled" or "recyclable" in an effort to capture sales from the newly environment-conscious public. For example, some paper manufacturers began marketing new lines of paper towels and toilet paper, saying they made these products only with recycled paper. And manufacturers of clothes, food products, toiletries, and other items also claimed their products used recycled containers or materials. Unfortunately, some of these companies recycled to a far lesser extent than they claimed. There was no way for consumers to know whose advertising was completely accurate.

Eventually, consumer organizations began investigating some of the claims companies made about recycling. They gave approval to the products whose labeling was accurate. Part of the

Concerned citizens gather trash that can be recycled into many useful items. Today, many people recognize recycling as both money saving and friendly to the environment.

problem, they found, was that different companies had different definitions and standards regarding recycling. The standards of some companies were much lower than those of others. Consumer organizations called for government regulations clearly defining what does and does not constitute a recycled product or material. Although these organizations continue to pressure the government, such regulations still do not exist.

A forklift stacks bales of aluminum cans into a mountain of metal. Today, the world's aluminum companies recycle nearly one-fourth of the total output of aluminum.

More materials recycled each year

Since the early 1970s, recycling has continued to expand around the world, both in industry and on the grassroots level—in homes, businesses, and communities. Today, governments, industries, and homeowners alike recognize recycling as both money saving and friendly to the environment. As in the past, industry continues to lead the way in the modern recycling movement. For example, to save energy and money, as well as to conserve natural resources, the world's combined aluminum companies now recycle 5 million tons a year. That is nearly a quarter of the world's total output of aluminum. Japan does the best in this respect, recycling 40 percent of its aluminum. Western European countries recycle 20 to 30 percent and the United States about 20 percent. The steel industry recycles even more of its product, often over 50 percent. Much of the recycled metal used by industry comes from scrapped cars. One average-sized car yields about three thousand pounds of iron, forty pounds of copper, fifty-four pounds of zinc, fifty pounds of aluminum, and twenty pounds of lead for recycling. The United States presently recycles over 4 million cars per year.

A boxcar-load of shredded aluminum cans is unloaded before being taken to a furnace for melting. Aluminum companies recycle about five million tons of aluminum annually.

Although home and community recycling cannot match industry's efforts in sheer tonnage, grassroots recycling programs have grown tremendously in size and importance in recent years. One reason for this growth is the passing of local and state laws requiring towns and cities to recycle part of their wastes. Since 1986, forty U.S. states have passed such laws. In 1989 alone, legislators and city officials in thirty-eight states created 134 new recycling laws. For example, in July 1989, a New York City law required the city to create programs to recycle 25 percent of its wastes in the following five years. And a state recycling law in California requires communities to reduce their volume of refuse by 25 percent by 1995 and 50 percent by the year 2000.

As a result of these laws and increased participation in recycling by residents and businesses, the country is recycling an increasing proportion of its wastes each year. The U.S. Environmental Protection Agency reported a 30 percent increase in the volume of refuse recycled in the country from 1986 to 1990 and expects the 1991-1995 period to show a similar increase. The United States currently recycles 55 percent, or more than 45 billion, of its aluminum cans. In addition, the country recycles about 25 percent of the 67 million tons of paper Americans use each year. Thousands of tons of glass and plastic are also recycled each month in the United States. Both are melted down and transformed into hundreds of different types of new products.

Something everyone can do

The recycling collection process has itself become big business. Thousands of liquor, grocery, and other stores across the country run redemption centers for aluminum and plastic cans and bottles. They offer customers a convenient place to drop off recyclables; then they sell these items to recyclers. Some states offer residents a cash recycling incentive: Consumers pay a five-cent or larger deposit for each can or bottle they purchase containing certain products such as soft drinks. When they return the cans or bottles, they receive their deposits back. In 1991, Americans received more than $1.2 billion by recycling these cans and bottles. Many of the remaining garbage landfills in the country now have recycling centers that accept newspapers, various plastics, glass, metal cans, and other recyclables. And more than one thousand five hundred communities now have a curbside recycling pickup service, often in conjunction with trash pickup. Trucks transport recyclables from homes, schools, and businesses to collection centers or recycling plants.

These widespread and diverse recycling operations employ a lot of people. Alcoa, a leading aluminum manufacturer, estimates that at least thirty thousand Americans are involved in aluminum recycling alone. Overall, the collecting, transporting, and converting of all types of recyclables employed close to one hundred thousand people nationwide in the early 1990s. And only about 15 percent of community-generated wastes were recycled during this period. Some experts estimate that if this country recycled 75 percent of these wastes, the number of people employed in recycling would rise to at least 375,000. So recycling not only helps alleviate the refuse problem, but also stimulates the economy by creating new jobs.

A modern rebirth

Thus, recycling, an old idea, has undergone a modern rebirth. People in the United States and many other countries find the idea appealing because it is a relatively simple process that reaps

A community recycling program makes recycling glass bottles easy and convenient for this restaurant owner and other small business owners.

large benefits. As Richard Zimmerman points out in *What Can I Do to Make a Difference?*, "Helping to solve the garbage glut by recycling is something every person can do each day without expending a lot of money and effort. Recycling offers the opportunity to decrease waste-disposal needs and costs while helping to combat global environmental problems." In simple terms, recycling makes sense.

A specially designed truck picks up recyclables at curbside. Such convenient curbside service encourages residents to recycle.

3

Recycling and the Environment

RECYCLING AFFECTS THE environment in a number of ways, both direct and indirect. The most obvious and beneficial ways are by helping to conserve natural resources, reducing pollution, and decreasing the need for incineration and landfills. But recycling is not the only solution to such environmental problems. For instance, making and using fewer disposable products in the first place also helps conserve resources and cut down on pollution. Other solutions include enforcing stricter antipollution laws; reducing the amount of waste in mining, drilling, logging, and manufacturing processes; and finding more efficient ways to use natural resources. Recycling is most effective when people use it in conjunction with these other solutions. Nevertheless, of all of these solutions, recycling has perhaps the greatest potential for creating dramatic results with very little effort.

Conserving valuable resources

Resource conservation is one area in which the effects of large-scale recycling can be especially dramatic. Modern civilization uses millions of barrels of oil, millions of trees, and hundreds of

(Opposite page) This dump is an eyesore and a threat to the environment. Poorly stored waste can seep into groundwater or drain into lakes and rivers. If such waste could be recycled, the danger it poses to the environment might be averted.

These and thousands of other oil wells pump petroleum from the earth for the world's energy needs. Recycling petroleum products, including motor oil and plastics, can help conserve dwindling oil supplies and also prevent pollution.

thousands of tons of metals each day. Unfortunately, existing supplies of these resources are neither limitless nor cheap. Many ecologists and oil experts warn that the world's major oil deposits may be used up in the next century. Though supplies of metals are more abundant, mining them requires a great deal of energy and money. In addition, extracting and processing oil and metals often causes various kinds of environmental damage and pollution. Recycling is one way to decrease both the demand for resources and the environmental problems associated with processing them.

Saving trees

Trees are another vital but limited resource that recycling helps conserve. Paper is made from trees, of course, and consumers around the world use hundreds of millions of tons of paper each year. Huge numbers of trees are needed to fuel this enormous demand for paper. For example, it takes seventy-five thousand trees to make the paper used to print just one issue of the Sunday *New York Times*. Thousands of other newspapers and magazines, as well as paper towels, napkins, and hundreds of other paper products, contribute to the felling of hundreds of millions of trees yearly in the United States alone. Although forestry companies plant new trees every year, trees take a long time to grow. And only so much land with adequate soil and rainfall is available to grow them on. So foresters often cannot plant trees fast enough to meet the yearly demand. Americans have already cut down and eliminated 95 percent of all the virgin forests that originally covered the continental United States. The remaining forests are rapidly disappearing.

How effective is the recycling of paper in saving trees? Recycling just one four-foot stack of newspapers could save a thirty-five- to forty-foot tree. Another way of looking at it: Recycling a ton of paper eliminates the need for three thousand seven hundred pounds of lumber. In 1992, Americans recycled about 25 percent of their newspapers and other paper products. That reduced the need for lumber by about 250 million trees, enough to fill a forest covering all six New England states.

While helping to conserve trees, recycling paper also reduces the environmental destruction associated with large-scale logging. Logging often causes severe soil erosion. The root systems of trees collect water and nutrients, helping to keep the soil rich and compact. When loggers re-

Old newspapers, shredded and baled, await processing at a recycling plant. Recycling paper conserves trees and prevents deforestation and soil erosion.

move trees and fail to plant new ones, the soil dries out and erodes. Without trees, water flows through the soil more quickly, causing rainwater drainage patterns to change. Floods and damage to nearby fisheries frequently result. In addition, large-scale logging destroys animal habitats. Although more responsible logging practices and increased replanting programs are partial solutions to these problems, recycling helps too. By saving 250 million trees each year, recycling can conserve the soil, water tables, and animal habitats associated with these trees.

Recycling paper also helps save water and reduce the pollution created in the paper-making process. Recycling just a single ton of paper, for example, saves about twenty-four thousand gallons of fresh water. Large amounts of water are needed to mix with and wash the wood pulp that eventually becomes paper. After the pulp is washed, bleaching agents and other potentially harmful chemicals remain in the wastewater the factory discharges into the environment. The more paper that is recycled, the less new paper has to be made. Therefore, fewer pollutants will enter lakes, streams, and water tables. Of course, even recycled paper must be processed and doing so uses water and chemicals. But making new paper out of recycled paper causes 50 percent less water pollution than making new paper directly from trees.

An alternative to burying refuse

Another way recycling helps the environment is by reducing the need for landfills and incinerators, which cause various kinds of pollution. The refuse thrown into landfills often contains harmful chemicals, and landfills frequently leak these substances into the soil. The chemicals can then seep into and pollute underground water tables

Paper mills are a principal source of water pollution. As this photograph of a Russian paper mill shows, such mills also contribute to air pollution.

that feed into streams and reservoirs.

Although many of the dangerous wastes leaked by landfills come from industrial dumping, individual consumers are also often to blame. The average American consumer generates about one hundred sixty pounds of household hazardous wastes each year. These substances include paint, detergents, cleaners, batteries, and motor oil. Instead of disposing of them safely in special metal or plastic containers, many people simply throw these wastes into their trash, which is eventually put in landfills. Some of the wastes seep into the water table. There, a very small amount of waste can often cause a great deal of contamination. For example, one gallon of motor oil can disperse in

Bulldozers compress mounds of garbage in a landfill to make room for more trash. Recycling helps reduce the millions of tons of waste dumped annually into landfills.

up to sixty-five thousand gallons of water, contaminating the water. Americans also discard about 2.6 billion household batteries each year into landfills. In time, the batteries leak acid into the soil and water, raising levels of highly toxic mercury in many areas of the country. These problems became so serious in the 1970s and 1980s that in September 1991 the EPA passed special antileakage regulations for landfills. One regulation requires that all new landfills have liners on their bottoms to contain leaking wastes. Another regulation requires landfills to have wells equipped with devices capable of detecting any groundwater contamination.

Unfortunately, these solutions do little to stop leakage in existing landfills that do not have liners and wells. Recycling, then, is one of the most effective ways of reducing toxic leakage. First, the more products such as oil and batteries that are recycled, the fewer hazardous wastes that make it into the landfills. Recycling also decreases the amount of landfill leakage by helping eliminate the need for so many landfills in the first place. Because paper products make up more than half of the waste materials in most landfills, recycling paper is especially important. Experts estimate that recycling 50 percent of the newspapers in the United States would reduce the flow of wastes into landfills by some 6 million tons. That amounts to 1,168,000 truckloads a year!

An alternative to incineration

Large-scale recycling also reduces the need for incinerators. According to John Young, writing in *World Watch* magazine, "The immediate environmental problems with incinerators . . . [are] air pollution and hazardous ash." Sulfur dioxide, carbon monoxide, arsenic, lead, and mercury are just a few of the many potentially dangerous sub-

stances released into the atmosphere during incineration. Engineers have addressed the problem by designing special filters, called scrubbers, for smokestacks. Although the scrubbers remove most of the pollutants from the smoke, the rapidly growing number of incinerators in the world still contributes heavily to air pollution. And after the refuse has been burned, the remaining ash is often toxic and it pollutes landfills and other sites where people dump it.

"Even more important than these concerns, however," says Young, "is incineration's destructive nature: it wastes materials and the energy used to produce them. . . . Spending on incineration necessarily comes at the expense of recy-

Incinerators such as this one in Pennsylvania reduce the volume of garbage in landfills but leave mounds of unsightly ash.

cling." In other words, it takes more money and energy to build and maintain an incinerator than to recycle the refuse burned in it.

Not all kinds of refuse are recyclable, so recycling cannot eliminate the need for all incinerators. But it can lessen that need and thereby reduce pollution, as well as save money and energy. Nevertheless, replacing a significant proportion of incinerators with recycling programs will take several years. Until recycling programs grow sufficiently large, incineration will remain a widespread practice. At present, the amount of money spent on incineration in the United States and many other countries, notably Japan, remains higher than the amount spent on recycling. According to Worldwatch Institute, eighteen U.S. states plan to spend eight to ten times more on incineration than on recycling until at least 1996.

Each year, however, more Americans recognize the benefits of recycling, and the recycling movement is growing steadily. According to Young and other experts, because it reduces pollution and is also economical, recycling is slowly becoming popular as an alternative to both incineration and landfills. Cynthia Pollock-Shea, of the World Resources Institute in Washington, D.C., states, "As landfill costs continue to rise due to space constraints [limitations] and stricter environmental regulations [to curb toxic leakage], and as the high . . . costs of incinerators and their pollution control technologies sap city budgets, the appeal of recycling will inevitably grow."

Necessary trade-offs

Despite its many benefits and its potential for helping solve environmental problems, recycling is not a perfect process. The ways various products are made and used are often very complicated, sometimes creating situations in which recycling has environmental drawbacks. "When you start digging into the nuts and bolts of how products are made and used, you learn . . . [that] there are complicated trade-offs that have to be made," says Norman L. Dean, executive director of Green Seal, a nonprofit organization that investigates environmental claims on product labels. The recycling process involves a number of such trade-offs. In a way, then, the old adage— that one must accept the bad with the good—applies to recycling. In order to enjoy the very real benefits of the process, people must be willing to live with the disadvantages.

One well-publicized recycling trade-off involves traditional cloth diapers and disposable, or nonreusable, plastic-lined diapers. Disposable diapers make up 80 to 85 percent of the $3 billion annual diaper market. American consumers throw

Greenpeace volunteers collect trash that litters a public recreation area. Much of the trash can be recycled.

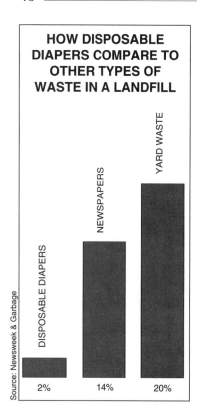

HOW DISPOSABLE DIAPERS COMPARE TO OTHER TYPES OF WASTE IN A LANDFILL

Source: Newsweek & Garbage

DISPOSABLE DIAPERS — 2%

NEWSPAPERS — 14%

YARD WASTE — 20%

away some 18 billion disposable diapers each year. That is enough to fill a large garbage truck every four minutes. The main problem with these throwaway diapers is that they require increasing amounts of space in landfills. They already take up 2 percent of the space in U.S. landfills, a huge proportion for a single product. And because the plastic takes hundreds of years to decompose, the diapers will remain in the ground for a long time. Therefore, over the years they will take up increasing amounts of landfill space, in turn increasing the need for more landfills.

Benefits of cloth diapers

On the other hand, cloth diapers are recyclable in the sense that they can be used over and over again. A cloth diaper can be laundered and reused an average of one hundred fifty times before it wears out. Obviously then, a single cloth diaper eliminates the need for one hundred fifty disposables. Consequently, in terms of being friendly to the environment, cloth diapers would appear to be the logical choice over disposable ones.

Yet that is not necessarily the case. Studies comparing the two types of diapers were conducted in the 1980s and early 1990s by independent labs in several states. These studies compared the amount of energy and water used, as well as the waste created, in the manufacture, use, and disposal of both products. Some studies found that it takes three times as much energy to make a cloth diaper. Also, in the manufacturing and laundering processes, cloth diapers add ten times as many pollutants to water systems. And because of constant rewashing, cloth diapers use up large amounts of fresh water. This contributes to the lowering of reservoirs and water tables, an increasingly serious problem in many areas of the country. By contrast, because disposable diapers

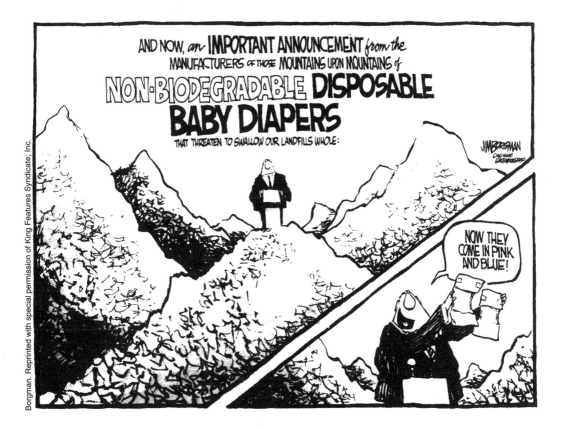

are never washed, they do not use up precious water supplies. Thus, recycling cloth diapers to help eliminate landfill problems requires the trade-off of using more energy and fresh water. For a consumer, then, choosing which type of diaper to use might hinge on which environmental issue is more important to him or her.

Recycling diapers

One possible solution to this dilemma is to recycle disposable diapers rather than throw them into landfills. That would eliminate the landfill problem and at the same time save energy and fresh water. But can plastic diapers be recycled? The Procter & Gamble Company, which makes various household products, is currently experimenting with the idea in a number of pilot programs. In one program, the company collected used disposable diapers from one thousand families in Seattle, Washington. The company then recycled the plastic into flowerpots and park benches. Procter & Gamble's goal is eventually to use such recycled plastic for making all of its liquid detergent and cleaner containers.

Packaging is another area in which recycling involves various trade-offs. Some types of packaging materials, especially paper and certain kinds of plastics, are easily recyclable. But other types of packaging are so difficult or expensive to

ELIMINATE THIS CONTAINER

BEFORE WE ELIMINATE THIS ONE!

WICKS

recycle that they are considered nonrecyclable, at least for now. One is polystyrene, used in making disposable fast-food containers and drinking cups. Another example is aseptic packaging, an especially germ-resistant kind of plastic often used for juice drinks. Recycling advocates argue that because these materials are not recycled, people should not use them. Instead, manufacturers should use bottles and containers made of glass, paper, or some other easily recycled material. Advocates say recyclable packaging will help the environment by reducing landfill and incinerator use.

Recycling advocates have lobbied hard to ban polystyrene and aseptic packaging until the materials can be recycled on a large scale. These efforts have been successful in changing several local food-packaging policies. For example, a number of cities, including Portland, Oregon, and Newark, New Jersey, banned polystyrene food packages in favor of paper packages in the late 1980s. And in 1991, Maine banned aseptic packages from shelves across the state.

Environmental trade-offs

Yet from an environmental standpoint, such policies involve certain trade-offs. First, the banned polystyrene containers take 30 percent less energy to manufacture than do their paper replacements. So, while Portland and Newark benefit by keeping polystyrene out of their landfills, paper manufacturers use up 30 percent more fuel and resources making the replacements. Making the polystyrene products also produces 46 percent less air pollution and 42 percent less water pollution than making the paper ones. The case is similar with aseptic packaging. Lynn Scarlett explains in *Consumer's Research Magazine*:

Filling aseptic packages requires about half the energy needed to fill glass bottles. Transporting the aseptic package from its manufacturer to the bottling site also dramatically reduces resource use, primarily fuel. For a given beverage volume, it takes fifteen times as many trucks to transport empty glass bottles as it does aseptic boxes. Because the end-product is lightweight, small and rectangular, the filled aseptic package can be more efficiently transported as well, using 35 percent less energy per unit than alternative glass packages. And the aseptic container is the only one in which dairy products can be packaged without requiring refrigeration—again saving energy.

Scarlett also points out that many of the nonrecyclable types of packages condemned by recycling advocates conserve resources by tightly and securely sealing food. This greatly reduces the amount of spoilage and breakage that might otherwise occur. Because of such packaging, says Scarlett, "The United States produces less food waste than anywhere else in the world except parts of Africa, where the threat of starvation means even rotten food is consumed." Therefore, despite the fact that these types of packaging cannot be recycled, they have measurable and important environmental benefits.

The truck trade-off

The fact that it takes more trucks to transport glass containers than aseptic packaging helps illustrate still another recycling trade-off. More trucks use more fuel and require more metals to build, both of which increase the drain on natural resources. More trucks also produce more exhaust fumes, which cause more air pollution. In addition to the extra trucks needed to haul glass instead of nonrecyclable packaging, curbside recycling also puts more trucks on the road. Many towns and private companies engaged in recy-

cling send one truck for the recyclables and another for the regular trash. This doubles the number of trucks, which significantly increases gasoline consumption and air pollution. A large number of trucks is also needed to haul recyclables from recycling centers to factories.

Alleviating this problem somewhat is the fact that recycling decreases the need for regular garbage trucks. The more refuse that is recycled, the smaller the volume that must be trucked to landfills. For every 1 million tons of refuse recycled each year, five hundred thirty-three fewer garbage trucks are needed. Nevertheless, the recycling industry puts thousands of trucks on the

The additional trucks needed for recycling pickup and transport increase the use of petroleum and steel, which subtracts from the overall environmental benefit of recycling.

road that would not be there otherwise. These use more than 200 million extra gallons of gasoline and over one hundred thousand extra tons of metals yearly. The truck trade-off: to reap the benefits of recycling, people must accept the increased demand for natural resources caused by the extra trucks.

Thus, there are some significant environmental trade-offs involved in the recycling process. Using recyclable products like cloth diapers, glass containers, and paper packaging can reduce landfill and incinerator use. But manufacturing and recycling these products often require more energy and fresh water supplies, and can increase water pollution. The question is: Do recycling's benefits outweigh its drawbacks? Most ecologists and environmentalists agree that they do. They are willing to accept the necessary trade-offs for the present and are confident that improving technology will eventually eliminate recycling's few but very real disadvantages. Explains Diane Duffy in *The Conservationist*, "Research about recycling and development of recycling technologies are expected to address . . . [environmental problems], given time. The information produced by these projects and by communities' experiences with recycling will expand the fund of shared wisdom [about effective recycling]."

4

Recycling Realities

PAUL NIELSEN, AN upholsterer from Barnstable, Massachusetts, has been diligently recycling for a number of years. Out of concern for the environment, once a week he takes his old newspapers, glass and plastic containers, and metal cans to a recycling collection center at his local landfill. For a long time, Nielson assumed that everything he brought to be recycled was actually recycled. One day in 1991 he was surprised to find that this is not always the case.

At the collection center, as he had done for years, Nielsen dumped his box of plastic bottles and containers into the bin labeled "plastics." That day, out of curiosity, he decided to stay for a while and watch the recycling attendants work. Instead of loading all of the plastics into a recycling truck, as Nielsen expected them to do, the attendants separated the plastics. They put some items into the truck but dumped many others right into the landfill. "What is the point of my recycling plastics," Nielsen asked an attendant, "if so much ends up in the landfill anyway?" The attendant explained that only some kinds of plastics are recycled on a large scale. This is because many other kinds are more difficult or expensive

(Opposite page) A recycling center in Seattle, Washington. Recycling companies can only profitably recycle certain materials. Many materials, especially certain types of plastics, are too expensive or difficult to recycle.

49

ADVENTURES IN RECYCLING

to recycle. Since there is little or no profit in recycling them, most plastics companies have not invested in the necessary equipment. They refuse to accept these items, which inevitably end up in landfills.

Paul Nielsen learned a valuable lesson that day. Like many other people, he had assumed that the amount of refuse recycled each year depends mainly on the number of people who recycle. If enough people showed concern and started recycling, he reasoned, all reusable refuse materials would eventually be recycled. Nielsen discovered an important reality: Concern for the environment and a willingness to recycle are not the only factors that influence how much and what kinds of materials get recycled. There are other factors, an important one being money. Often, if recycling certain items is not profitable, fewer of those items will be recycled, regardless of environmental concerns.

Making a profit from old newspapers

A clear example of how the marketplace influences recycling is the case of old newspapers. Concern about environmental pollution and vanishing forests prompted many communities to begin recycling newspapers in the late 1960s and early 1970s. These communities soon learned that recycling newspapers was not only environmentally friendly, but also profitable. This was because many paper mills, finding that buying recycled paper was cheaper than processing new paper from trees, were eager to buy recycled paper. There was, therefore, a demand in the marketplace for recycled newspapers. That demand could be translated into a profit, as the residents of Madison, Wisconsin, learned when the city opened the first large-scale municipal newspaper-recycling project in 1968. Explains journalist and author Katie Kelly in her book, *Garbage*:

> The plan was to have Madison householders separate their newspapers, some 170 tons, out of their garbage each week. These were to be bundled, tied, and placed at curbside for pickup. A special hopper was designed for the garbage trucks, a metal rack under the body of each compactor truck. Once they were installed, newspapers were collected, sorted, and hauled to a dealer who had contracted to buy the waste paper from the city. He, in turn, sold it to a nearby paper mill. . . . By early 1971, the city was actually making a net profit of $2.06 per ton. In the first two-year period some 3,242 tons of old newspapers had been collected in Madison, most of which went right back into the economy as new newsprint.

As the demand for recycled newspapers grew, many other cities across the country followed Madison's lead and instituted similar newspaper-

Newspaper recycling was so successful in the late 1980s that more old newspaper was collected than could be sold and profitably recycled.

recycling operations. More and more Americans began recycling newspapers during the 1970s and 1980s.

Changes in demand

Eventually, however, the marketplace demand for old newspapers changed. One reason was that some companies that supplied trees to paper mills began to compete with paper recyclers. By making it cheaper for the manufacturers to make virgin paper from trees, the forestry companies slowed the demand for recycled newspapers in some areas in the 1980s. Some paper manufacturers then reasoned that their plants for processing old newspapers were adequate to meet the existing demand. So, to save money, they decided not to build new plants until demand substantially increased. They also built few new de-inking facilities. These are essential to processing recycled newspapers because the ink must be removed from the paper before new, usable paper can be made. Thus, competition in the marketplace caused both the demand for and the capacity to process old newspapers to level off in some areas.

Other factors also affected the demand for recycled newspapers. For instance, some paper manufacturers saw that the volume of recycled papers varied from month to month and from one part of the country to another. On the other hand, the supply of new wood pulp was constant and more predictable. Thus some manufacturers, unsure about steady supplies of recycled newspapers, considered building new facilities to process old papers economically risky.

Another factor affecting demand was the unwillingness of manufacturers to buy all of the old newspapers collected. The quality of the papers influenced this decision. "Recycling programs have difficulty marketing newspaper because the materials do not meet the specifications of their market," explains Will Ferretti of the New York State Department of Economic Development, Energy Conservation Services Unit. Often, old newspapers are exposed to dampness, sunlight, or wind, all of which affect the color and durability of the papers when they are recycled. Also, most recycling programs do not require that people remove the glossy inserts from newspapers during recycling. These inserts contain dyes that ruin the reprocessed paper, so all papers containing inserts are rejected by manufacturers. Still another problem is newspapers collected in grocery bags or tied with twine. The manufacturers are less likely to accept these because they do not want to spend the extra money to remove the bags and twine.

Paper awaiting recycling must be separated, cleaned, and treated before it can be reused. Each step takes time and costs money. Often, companies find it easier and cheaper to use virgin wood pulp to make new paper.

In the early 1990s, some areas of the United States had such a glut of old newspapers that recyclers had to pay paper manufacturers to take newspapers off their hands.

Thus, because of factors like economic competition, uncertainties about supplies, and the quality of the papers, the marketplace dictated the volume of newspapers that could be profitably reprocessed in the 1980s. While there was still a demand for recycled newspapers by manufacturers, by the late 1980s that demand had leveled off in many parts of the United States. At the same time, however, the volume of newspapers being collected for recycling in many parts of the country substantially increased. People were collecting many more newspapers than the marketplace demanded. Therefore, in the late 1980s and early 1990s there was a glut, or oversupply, of old newspapers in some states and cities. The situation was worst in the Northeast, perhaps because the sheer volume of old newspapers collected in that highly populous area is larger than in most other areas.

An uncertain future

What happens to these stockpiled old newspapers? Unfortunately, they cannot simply be stored indefinitely and recycled later, when and if demand for them increases. The paper fibers decay in time, making the old newspapers unfit for recycling within one to two years. Therefore, if not sold promptly, these papers no longer have market value. In fact, they often have negative value. For example, in October 1989, instead of the usual situation, in which manufacturers pay recyclers for the papers, recyclers had to pay manufacturers up to ten dollars a ton to take the old papers off recyclers' hands. By March 1992, the price per ton had fallen even further, to minus thirty-two dollars at some times. Many communities were unwilling to pay so much just to make sure newspapers got recycled. So many of the extra newspapers collected ended up in landfills or incinerators.

Thus, even though many people diligently recycle their newspapers, not all of those papers get reprocessed into new paper. As long as the marketplace demands a limited amount of recycled newspapers, this situation will not change much. Most experts are unsure when demand for old newspapers will begin rising again. Says Allen Blakey of the National Solid Wastes Management Association, "There are a number of new mills and de-inking facilities presently being built and capacity [to process old papers] will grow in the next few years. So, the situation may eventually improve. But no one knows for sure." One reason for the uncertainty is that building new facilities takes so long. According to Thomas Kraner of the American Paper Institute, a New York-based group that collects and provides information about the paper industry, getting all the necessary permits and constructing a paper-processing plant takes three to four years. There is no way to tell whether supplies of old newspapers and other market factors will be the same when the plant is completed.

Legal roadblocks

The profit motive and other aspects of the marketplace are not the only factors that influence what and how much is recycled. Sometimes, technical and legal problems arise that discourage the recycling of certain items.

For example, the future of battery recycling is uncertain. People have routinely recycled batteries for years, but public fears that the process might be unsafe are creating difficulties for companies that recycle batteries. This is a problem because the fewer batteries that are recycled, the more that get thrown away. And disposing of batteries in traditional ways—landfills and incineration—is a proven environmental hazard. Diane Duffy explains:

> Lead-acid batteries, the type used for starting cars and boats, typically contain 18 to 20 pounds of lead. Dry cell and button batteries, used to power flashlights, watches and radios, contain cadmium, nickel, and mercury. The heavy metals in batteries are toxic and long-lasting, but pose no threat to people or the environment when the sealed batteries are in use. However, in a landfill where the seal can be broken, batteries can release acid and metals into the environment.

Because of the toxic threat of these heavy metals, some state agencies are considering regulations. These rules would prohibit landfills from accepting used vehicle batteries. Burning batter-

ies is no better than dumping them because traces of the heavy metals exist in the waste ash that incinerators release into the air. In 1988, dry-cell, mercury, and vehicle batteries were classified as untreatable wastes, meaning there was no effective way of treating them to make them less toxic.

For many years, the logical alternative to these unsafe methods of dealing with old batteries was recycling. Most of the toxic metals in batteries can be removed in the recycling process. For example, according to the Battery Council Interna-

Disposing of batteries in landfills is a proven environmental hazard.

tional, or BCI, a trade association representing 95 percent of U.S. battery manufacturers and recyclers, all of the lead in a lead battery is recyclable. In 1990, the EPA estimated that about 80 percent of all lead batteries in the United States were recycled.

Despite this impressive recycling record, the rate of recycling for used car batteries is decreasing. Part of the problem is that the EPA passed strict rules in the 1980s about cleaning up water sources near battery-recycling facilities. In the early 1990s, fearing they would be fined or forced to clean up polluted lakes and streams,

An inspector makes a record of old batteries awaiting recycling or disposal. Recent laws to prevent pollution from battery-recycling plants have caused many such plants to shut down.

some battery recyclers closed down. With fewer facilities in operation, fewer batteries were recycled. Compounding the dilemma, when recyclers try to build new facilities, they often encounter opposition from communities. Many residents fear having a plant that might leak toxic metals in their neighborhoods or towns. So they pressure local officials to refuse the recyclers the necessary building permits.

Thus, because of the growing number of regulations and legal roadblocks, an item that could be recycled more is being recycled less. Most battery manufacturers and recyclers believe the solution to the problem is to educate the public. Many of these firms are lobbying the federal government to institute informational programs about the benefits of battery recycling.

Another factor that influences the amount of materials recycled is public confusion about the best ways to help alleviate the present garbage crisis. A majority of people in the United States and other developed countries probably know about recycling. They realize that it can help reduce the volume of refuse in landfills and incinerators. But recycling takes a certain amount of effort that many people are reluctant to expend. Sometimes they are attracted to other methods that promise environmental benefits with little or no effort.

Biodegradable garbage bags

One example is the use of biodegradable plastic garbage bags, introduced during the 1980s. Regular plastic bags take hundreds, perhaps thousands, of years to biodegrade, or break down into simpler substances via the action of natural processes. As a result, the garbage inside a sealed bag can linger in a landfill for a long time. This bag not only takes up space, but also increases

Plastic trash bags filled with garbage litter a river bank. Because plastic does not break down easily this garbage could lie here for decades.

the risk that the refuse will eventually resurface somehow and litter the countryside. Biodegradable bags, on the other hand, break down more quickly. According to their manufacturers, this allows their contents to break down more rapidly, saving landfill space and reducing future litter problems. Many people think that using biodegradable bags is a solution to the national refuse crisis.

But biodegradable bags may not be a significant solution. Although they biodegrade quicker than regular bags, they still take at least a few years to break down. Also, their degree of degradability depends on the amount of air and sunlight they are exposed to. When buried in landfills, they may break down much more slowly or not at all.

Some experts believe the problem is not that people use biodegradable bags, but rather that many people choose them instead of recycling. According to Karl Kamena, a spokesperson for the Dow Chemical Company, biodegradable products appear to offer people an easy solution to garbage problems. "Degradability sounds better than recycling," says Kamena, "because peo-

New recycling technologies are currently being developed. This plant recycles polystyrene foam used to make fast-food containers and disposable coffee cups.

ple don't have to do anything." Industry expert Norman H. Nosenchuck agrees. He says that garbage problems can be alleviated much more effectively by recycling than by using biodegradable bags. Instead of spending money to develop biodegradable products, says Nosenchuck, "We should concentrate on the technology of recycling polystyrene, such as fast food packages, coffee cups, and egg cartons. . . . That would be a genuine contribution to the recycling effort."

No one knows how many people who use biodegradable bags would practice recycling if the bags were not available. But there is little doubt that many people who are genuinely concerned about the environment do not recycle because they think using the bags is an equally

The relative ease and safety of recycling aluminum make it a profitable venture and a recycling success story.

good alternative. So a great deal of refuse that might otherwise be recycled ends up in landfills. Thus, people's concerns about the environment and their willingness to help do not always result in the growth of recycling programs.

Although experts expect recycling to grow in popularity in coming decades, that growth is likely to be slow and sometimes unpredictable. As Diane Duffy points out, large-scale recycling by consumers is still a relatively new industry, and the markets and technology are still changing and growing. As a result, says Duffy, "What looks like a recycling solution often turns out to be the beginning of another issue." Such recycling realities as changing markets, public fears about the hazards of battery recycling, and the biodegradability issue will undoubtedly continue to influence what and how much gets recycled for several years to come.

5

Searching for Innovative Ideas

STANDARD RECYCLING PROGRAMS, such as those that collect and reuse glass, newspapers, and plastic and aluminum cans and bottles, are widespread in the United States and many other countries. Experts predict that these programs will expand as more people begin recycling and as more markets for recycled products open up. Industries, especially those that produce aluminum, steel, and other metals, continue to recycle large volumes of materials, as they have for many decades. These industries regularly strive to recycle more because it is profitable for them to do so.

Although these familiar, well-established operations are effective, some communities, businesses, and industries constantly seek ways to make them more effective. For instance, some communities are not satisfied merely with setting up recycling centers for those residents interested in participating. These communities want to convince *all* of their residents to participate in recycling. Their goal is to make refuse disposal manageable and to earn income for the community in the process. Such ambitious efforts inevitably require the introduction of innovative ideas and methods.

In addition to improving existing programs, re-

(Opposite page) Old automobile tires are loaded onto a truck for transport to a reprocessing plant. This and other recycling efforts may lead the way to a cleaner future.

searchers seek new ways to recycle familiar products and materials. They also search for ways to recycle materials not normally considered recyclable. The immediate goal of this research is to expand the volume of materials recycled yearly. The long-range goal of some of these experiments is to lead eventually to whole new recycling industries. In time, researchers hope, creative, new approaches to recycling will eliminate the garbage dilemma and ensure a significantly cleaner environment.

Worries about refuse-disposal problems and environmental pollution have led some communities to strive for massive citizen participation in recycling. These programs are inspired by studies indicating that community recycling could eliminate

A worker uses a giant, motorized pincer to move a 15-ton bar of aluminum made from recycled beverage cans. The recycled aluminum will make about 750,000 new cans.

most of the need for landfills and incinerators. One of the best known of these studies was conducted in the late 1980s by researchers at the Center for the Biology of Natural Systems, or CBNS, at Queens College in New York City. CBNS estimated that large-scale community recycling could eliminate as much as 85 to 90 percent of the solid wastes now being buried or burned. A special pilot program conducted in 1987 by the town of East Hampton, New York, yielded similar estimates. One hundred volunteer families participated in intensive recycling and achieved a recycling rate of 84 percent. By comparison, most towns and cities with standard recycling programs recycle only 10 to 30 percent of their refuse.

Can recycling programs work?

But there is a big difference between one hundred families and an entire city. Can the kind of program conducted in East Hampton work on a much larger scale? Community leaders in Seattle, Washington, believe it can. In 1988, Seattle began a recycling program designed to reduce and eventually eliminate a serious refuse crisis. In 1986, it became clear that the city's only landfill was nearly out of space and would have to be closed. One solution proposed was to build an incinerator, but the community rejected that idea in favor of an ambitious recycling plan. The goal of the plan is to reduce the amount of refuse requiring disposal by 60 percent by the year 1998.

In implementing the plan, Seattle introduced a number of innovative ideas. First, the city provided an incentive to recycle by charging residents hefty fees for refuse pick up. The charge was $13.55 per month for the first can of refuse and $5 for each additional can. The more materials residents recycled, the fewer garbage cans they filled and the less they had to pay. The city further en-

couraged residents to reduce their waste generation and recycle by offering a special "Mini-can"
rate. Those who could fit all of their nonrecyclable materials into one small can were charged
23 percent less than the standard one-can rate.

Recycling through private companies

Another innovative idea Seattle initiated was to
keep the city out of the actual process of collecting recyclables. Buying the trucks and building
the facilities needed, as well as paying salaries to
collection workers, would have been extremely
expensive. Instead, reports Lynn Scarlett, "The
city decided to contract with private companies to
collect, transport, sort, and market recyclables."
Such companies already have trucks, facilities,
and workers in place. Also, because private companies compete with each other for jobs, they
charge lower rates and can get the job done more
cheaply than the city could. Seattle used these
companies to its best advantage. Scarlett explains:

> To benefit from the cost-containing effects of
> competition, the city specified that no contractor
> could serve more than one-half of the city. More-
> over, having reviewed the variety of different [re-
> cycling] systems . . . Seattle officials decided it
> was unclear which of the many collection systems
> was superior. Consequently, they did not specify
> how the private recycling service must operate but
> rather allowed the bidder to design the system. . . .
> Ultimately, the city awarded contracts to two pri-
> vate bidders—one to serve the south end of the
> city and the other the north. Each operates with its
> own collection plan, though the two services share
> some common features.

The results of Seattle's experiment in intensive
recycling have already been spectacular. By the
end of 1988 alone, approximately 67 percent of the
city's residents participated in recycling. And the
amount of refuse going into the local landfill was

Community recycling programs like this curbside pickup service will continue to play an important part in future recycling efforts.

reduced by some three thousand one hundred tons each month. By the end of 1989, Seattle's overall recycling rate was 37 percent, the highest of any city of its size in the country. City officials are confident they will meet their projected goal of substantially reducing refuse generation in the 1990s.

Seattle's success story has inspired other communities. For example, in the early 1990s the town of High Bridge, New Jersey, introduced a per-bag rate system similar to Seattle's. In the first year, High Bridge experienced a large increase in recycling activity and a 25 percent reduction in residential trash. Remarked one High Bridge resident, "I've been [recycling] for years, but many of my friends and neighbors said they

Public protests and other factors prompted McDonald's to switch from polystyrene to paper packaging.

couldn't be bothered. But now they bother because its hitting them in the pocketbook." Other communities that have tried per-bag rates with promising results are Woodstock, Illinois; Lansing, Michigan; and Perkasie, Pennsylvania.

Recycling at the golden arches

Communities are not the only places where people are trying out new kinds of recycling programs. Some large businesses have undertaken massive recycling efforts. These efforts often require daring approaches to recycling. One of the largest and most impressive examples is the program instituted by the McDonald's Corporation in the early 1990s. Called McDonald's McRecycle USA, the program is committed to introducing recycling into every aspect of McDonald's fast-food business. In this way, say company spokespersons, McDonald's hopes to set an example for businesses and individuals across the country and around the world.

One innovative idea in the McRecycle USA program has changed the way the company builds its restaurants. McDonald's now uses a high proportion of recycled construction products. These products range from various kinds of particle boards to concrete blocks made with recycled plastic instead of sand. The company plans to buy 100 million dollars' worth of recycled products for use in building, or remodeling, its restaurants during the 1990s. The company has also begun using recycled paper in many of its paper products. In addition, the company now ships and stores its soft drink syrups in reusable tanks rather than in throwaway cardboard containers. This step alone saves some 68 million pounds of packaging a year.

A move to paper wrappers

Perhaps the most widely publicized aspect of the McRecycle USA program was McDonald's decision to stop using polystyrene foam to wrap its foods. The familiar "clamshell" containers for hamburgers, Big Macs, and fries were replaced by paper containers. The Environmental Defense Fund, a New York-based organization that sponsors recycling programs, helped McDonald's plan the switchover to paper. The two organizations were disturbed by the fact that polystyrene can emit dangerous chemicals, both during production and later on in landfills. McDonald's was using twenty-two pounds of polystyrene a day in each of its eleven thousand locations worldwide. That is a total of two hundred forty-two thousand

A McDonald's executive compares paper packaging with foam sandwich containers.

pounds of polystyrene a day, or more than 88 million pounds a year! The move to paper wrappers will do more than help the environment. Because the paper is recyclable, the company may be able to reduce its yearly trash volume by as much as 90 percent.

Setting an example for millions

Another business that has recently initiated many innovative and effective approaches to recycling is the entertainment industry, based mainly in the Los Angeles area. For one thing, many television shows depict characters practicing recycling as a natural, everyday activity. Shows like "The Golden Girls," "Murphy Brown," "Empty Nest," and "Blossom" regularly show characters tossing glass bottles into recycling bins or shopping with reusable canvas bags.

Says TV producer Tony Thomas, "We just show by example what can be done without putting in dialogue. We just show by actions."

Because these shows reach millions of homes, they help promote the idea of recycling nationwide and even in foreign countries that carry the shows. Andy Spahn, president of California's Environmental Media Association, a clearinghouse of environmental information, views these efforts as valuable. "The entertainment industry is in a unique position to reach millions of people in a way grassroots movements and politicians can't," says Spahn.

Recycling at film studios

Another way the entertainment industry contributes to the recycling effort is by organizing special recycling programs at various film studios. According to estimates by Los Angeles city officials, the eleven major studios, including independent movie and TV producers, generate fifteen thousand tons or more of waste a year. In the late 1980s and early 1990s, many studios made a concerted effort to reduce these wastes by recycling.

For example, one of the biggest sources of throwaway materials at the studios is used film sets. Once filmmakers are finished with a set, they usually tear it down to make way for a new one. In the past, most used set materials were just discarded. Today, many studios are finding uses for these materials. Culver City, located near Los Angeles, now offers the studios reduced rates for separating clean wood from wood contaminated by paint and nails. Both kinds of wood get recycled. The clean wood is made into mulch for gardens or sawdust for horseback-riding stables; the contaminated wood becomes fuel for an electrical plant. A private group interested in film set recycling, called Safe Sets, works with many set de-

New ideas for recycling tires include using them for offshore fish- and oyster-breeding programs as well as in the production of new tires.

signers. The group helps take down the sets, then finds other uses for the parts. For instance, in the summer of 1991, Safe Sets donated a mechanized set made from recycled film sets to the California Youth Theatre for a production of *Little Shop of Horrors*. Comments Joan Satt of Los Angeles's Integrated Solid Waste Management Office, "The goal is to take these things that were once waste and make use of them in a real constructive way."

Making old items useful

In addition to sets, most studios recycle a host of other items. For example, Paramount Studios recycles computer paper and donates old office equipment to organizations that help the needy. The Warner Brothers studio recycles light bulbs, metal paint cans, and plastic film containers. The studio also gives costume remnants to a local company that transforms them into clothing and bedding. The studio even donates leftover paint, which would normally by disposed of as hazardous waste, to antigraffiti groups and schools.

While many communities and businesses introduce innovative, effective programs to recycle unusual materials, researchers continue to search for new ways to recycle familiar products. In the past, some products have been recycled only in wartime or not at all. For example, tens of millions of tires from junked cars pile up in junkyards each year. Anxious to stop this waste, a number of organizations have found ways to use the old tires. For instance, the fishing industry has successfully experimented with dropping tires onto the ocean floor in coastal waters. There, several species of fish use the tires as breeding grounds. Similarly, researchers working for the state of Florida have successfully bred oysters in old tires.

The Goodyear Rubber Company has pioneered a method of using ground-up scrap tires to produce carbon black, one of the most important ingredients in tires. One old tire provides about the right amount of carbon black to make one new tire. "There is an outstanding example of recycling," comments a Goodyear spokesperson, "a continuous circle involving the production of new tires, the total destruction of old tires, and use of the materials in new tire production." Goodyear estimates that as many as 60 million old tires can be recycled each year using this process.

Recycling and the construction industry

Researchers have also found ways to use recycled materials to make building blocks for various types of construction. One example is the use of ground-up plastic as a replacement for some of the sand in concrete. This kind of concrete is lighter and more crack-resistant than the standard kind. Another kind of recycled building block was introduced by researchers at the U.S. Bureau of Mines. According to journalist Katie Kelly, these lightweight blocks are made

> by molding concrete around cores of compressed automobile scrap. Car bodies are burned to get rid of flammable materials—plastics, seat stuffing, wood paneling—then the scrap metal residue is cut into sections and compressed into cubes, which are each encased in two inches of concrete. The heat generated during the . . . process is used to steam-cure the concrete coat.

Researchers are also studying the possibility of recycling polystyrene, although most polystyrene is not presently recycled. Eight major plastics manufacturers, including the Amoco Chemical Company, pooled their resources in the late 1980s to study ways of recycling polystyrene. Their goal is to recycle 25 percent of all disposable polystyrene products by the year 1995. In addition to Amoco's transformation of polystyrene containers into cafeteria trays and office products, there have been other successful experiments with this substance. In 1988, researchers used nine thousand pounds of plastic "lumber" made from discarded polystyrene in the John Innskeep Environmental Learning Center in Portland, Oregon. The special lumber became the construction material for park benches, walkways, and signs. The ongoing research at Amoco and other companies keeps alive the hope that someday most or all discarded polystyrene will be recycled.

An impossible goal?

Discarded tires, cars, plastics, and polystyrene make up much of the refuse that chokes landfills and junkyards. So the innovative methods found to recycle these materials are important and exciting. But what about the landfills and junkyards themselves? Once they fill up and close, these dumps are, in a sense, discarded, just like the in-

In only six weeks, the aluminum scraps from used beverage cans can be reprocessed into shiny, new cans ready for refilling.

As used polystyrene containers travel up a conveyor belt behind him, a recycling plant worker inspects the small, plastic pellets into which the containers are processed. The pellets are then used to make new plastic products.

dividual items of refuse within them. Most dumps remain eyesores or potential environmental hazards for decades. Is there a way to recycle entire dumps, to transform them into something safe and useful?

Just such a large-scale recycling feat was accomplished in Riverview, Michigan, near Detroit. Riverview is conducting a unique decades-long experiment that began in the 1970s. The town had two goals. The first was to create a landfill that, when in operation, would be profitable. The second goal was to make the landfill recyclable, so that even after it closed it would be both useful and profitable.

Riverview's experimental dump opened in

1971. It is equipped with a special liner at the bottom to keep chemicals from leaking down into soil and water tables. It also has facilities for recovering methane gas emitted by the rotting garbage. Technicians convert the gas into electricity, which provides power for the buildings at the landfill. Riverview also invited sixteen neighboring communities to dump refuse in its landfill. The towns dump an average total of five thousand cubic yards of refuse per day, for which they pay fees to Riverview. The money the town made during the dump's first two decades of operation paid for a $250,000 fire engine, funding school and senior citizen programs, and construction of a new city hall.

Eventually, a mound in one part of the landfill grew higher than the rest of the landfill. Riverview residents began referring to the hill of refuse as Mount Trashmore. In the 1980s, the town converted Mount Trashmore into a recreation area. Workers covered the mound with dirt and planted grass on it. Over this they built a ski

Even landfills are recyclable. An aerial view of the recreation area that was built on a specially constructed landfill known as Mount Trashmore.

slope and a golf course, which attract both residents and out-of-towners and earn a profit. Meanwhile, the remainder of the landfill still operates, and local officials estimate it has another twenty-five years of life left. During that time, the town plans to convert more mounds of refuse like Mount Trashmore.

Riverview's remarkable achievement has set an example for other communities. Towns all across the nation and in some foreign countries are studying the Mount Trashmore project and considering similar large-scale recycling projects of their own. But Riverview's experiment has shown more than how to recycle a landfill. By tackling and successfully accomplishing its seemingly impossible goal, the town proved that people can recycle almost anything if they really want to. Riverview showed that the keys to any effective recycling program are a strong desire to achieve the goal, finding innovative ways to implement the program, and careful planning.

Children play and water birds congregate at a Virginia Beach, Virginia, park that was once a garbage dump. As a new century dawns, human inventiveness will have to find ways of living with limited resources. Recycling will undoubtedly be one of those ways.

Appendix

Three Recycling Programs

MANY RECYCLING PROGRAMS and activities operate routinely in the United States and many other countries. Some programs involve homes and gardens, others schools and offices, and still others various kinds of businesses and industries. Following are three step-by-step guides to recycling programs consumers can easily practice every day. This information comes from recycling experts and organizations. In addition to tips on recycling, the program descriptions contain information on how to encourage others to recycle and how to help get recycling legislation passed. For more information, call and ask for brochures from the Environmental Defense Fund, (800) CALL-EDF; the EPA Office of Solid Wastes, (800) 424-9346 or (202) 260-4687; the American Paper Institute, (212) 340-0600; or an appropriate organization listed in Organizations to Contact following this appendix.

Precycling

Precycling is a helpful preliminary step in the recycling process. The two key words in precycling are *reduce* and *reuse*. By reducing the amount of unneeded products and packaging they collect, people can, in turn, reduce the amount of waste that they have to throw away or recycle. Often, reducing waste can be accomplished simply by shopping sensibly. By reusing many items, people can further reduce their trash output. Following is a brief list of "reduce and reuse" tips. A more complete list appears in the helpful book, *A Complete Guide to Recycling at Home* by Gary D. Branson.

1. Carry groceries in a reusable canvas or cotton-mesh bag. That reduces the use of both paper and plastic bags.

2. Choose products with minimum packaging. Remember that at least 50 percent of the wastes generated in homes comes from packaging.

3. Buy in bulk. One large container produces less trash than three or four small ones.

4. Buy concentrates and add water. Also, buy refillable containers.

5. Shred, wad, or crumple junk mail or nonrecyclable paper and use it for cushioning breakable items in packages you send in the mail.

6. Photocopy on both sides of the paper.

7. Use plastic produce bags to line small trash cans or wrap sandwiches.

8. Search out permanent replacements for disposable products such as pens, razor blades, and batteries. Buy rechargable batteries for most uses.

9. Cut back on the junk mail you receive by writing to the Mail Preference Service, Direct Marketing Association, 11 West 42nd Street, P.O. Box 3861, New York, NY 10163-3861. Ask that your name not be sold to mailing-list companies.

10. Check out which materials are being recycled in your area before buying; i.e., cut down on buying glass-packaged products if glass recycling is unavailable.

11. Buy quality products and take care of them. This not only reduces your cost of living, but also decreases the amount of materials you throw away.

12. Get refunds whenever possible. Return defective merchandise to the place you bought it rather than let items sit around unused and eventually get thrown away.

13. Sell or donate cast-off clothes instead of trashing them.

14. Write letters to your state legislature asking for better enforcement of litter laws on highways.

Becoming a committed recycler

Regularly recycling items like glass and plastic bottles, plastic containers, and metal cans is an excellent approach to saving resources. If enough people recycle these things, the volume of waste burned and buried will decrease considerably. For those who wish to do even more, to become totally committed recyclers, the following tips are helpful. Most of these, as well as hundreds of other facts and suggestions about recycling, can be found in Richard Zimmerman's excellent book, *What Can I Do to Make a Difference? A Positive Action Sourcebook.*

1. Recycle the items you use at home as much as possible. Encourage friends and neighbors to do the same.

2. Look into home composting. Yard wastes constitute about 20 percent of the trash Americans generate, yet all such lawn clippings, soil, and leaves can be composted. Composting can turn this garbage into nutrient-rich soil for healthier, more attractive lawns and gardens.

3. Encourage people in your community and workplace to recycle.

4. Ask local officials if they support recycling. If they do not, urge them to do so. Ask your local and state representatives to supply you with the names and addresses of local agencies that deal with recycling.

5. Start your own recycling center. Such an endeavor can be both profitable and enjoyable. To learn how, see "How to Start a Recycling Center" by the California Solid Waste Management Board or *How to Start a Neighborhood Recycling Center,* c/o the Ecology Center Bookstore, 2701 College Ave., Berkeley, CA 94705.

6. Vote for recycling legislation, and support legislators who favor recycling.

7. Donate old or worn-out clothes and household items to a local thrift store, such as those run by the Salvation Army.

8. Buy products made from recycled materials.

9. Buy products packaged in materials that can easily be recycled, such as glass, paper, and aluminum.

10. "Ask for paper instead of plastic," says Richard Zimmerman. "Some supermarkets encourage shoppers to bring in their own bags and give a refund of several cents for each bag used. Some companies that make canvas shopping bags include the Coalition for Recycled Waste, Treesavers of Solana Beach, CA, Save A Tree Co. of Berkeley, CA, and CO-OP America."

11. Zimmerman also urges people to "participate in plastics education programs. . . . Posters and signs on supermarket shelves urging shoppers to avoid excessive or nonrecyclable packaging, labels indicating recyclability, pro-paper bag rallies, and local media campaigns have all been tried at the local level. Contact the Pennsylvania Resources Council (44 East Front Street, Media, PA, 19063, (215) 565-9131) for further information."

Organizing a paper drive

One of the best ways to help reduce the amount of waste in landfills is to recycle newspapers. Groups can organize drives to collect newspapers. Following are some general steps recommended by the American Paper Institute. More details about this and other paper-recycling programs are available on request from the Institute. (See Organizations to Contact list for the address.)

Step 1—Establish a market for old newspapers.

Before beginning the paper drive, ask a local wastepaper firm if it buys old newspapers in your area and how much it pays for them. These firms are usually listed in the Yellow

Pages under "Waste Paper." There may be more than one firm in the area, so it is best to contact several to get the best quotes on prices.

Step 2—Motivate the group.

Encourage group members to participate in the paper drive. Such drives need the full support of volunteers because collecting paper takes many hours and often requires weekend work. The leader can pick a committee to call, encourage, and schedule the members of the group.

Step 3—Define the collection area.

Testing the collection program in a small area first is the best approach. Major problems can be identified and eliminated in advance. Later, you can repeat the process on a larger scale in other areas or neighborhoods. Choose the first collection area by using a zoning map from the city or county engineer's office. Such maps show streets and individual lots and give a rough idea of the population in the collection area.

Step 4—Choose the right collection method.

You can employ curbside collection, in which the collection teams pick up papers people leave out on the curb. Or people can bring their papers to a convenient central location, such as a school or church. There, the collection teams help unload the papers from the participants' vehicles.

The method used depends on the number of team members. It also depends on what equipment—cars, trucks, bins, and so on—is available. The size of the collection area is also a factor.

Step 5—Assign collection teams and equipment.

After establishing the area and picking the collection method, the next step is to divide the area into several sections of approximately equal size. Then assign a collection team and equipment to each section. In curbside collections, cars or trucks should move down each street within an assigned area and collect papers. In central site locations, set up one large container, bin, or truck. Remove twine, paper bags, and colored inserts before taking newspapers to the recycler.

Step 6—Get publicity.

The American Paper Institute makes these suggestions:

> Once the program is fully organized, inform the residents in the collection area that they should save their old newspapers for the upcoming drive. The type of publicity campaign depends on the size of the collection area and the frequency of the paper drives. If you expect to cover at least one-third of the city, you probably can expect some cooperation from news media in the form of newspaper articles and, perhaps, public service television and radio announcements. If your collection area is smaller, take your request directly to the residents via handbills delivered to each home. All printed materials should include the name of your group, the date of the collection, the place, the types of papers being collected, and how they should be bundled. Regardless of your situation, allow at least one month between the first announcement of your drive and your initial collection date—to enable residents to begin separating and storing their old newspapers.

Organizations to Contact

Alliance to Save Energy
1925 K St., NW
Suite 206
Washington, DC 20006
(202) 857-0666

A nonprofit coalition of business, government, and consumer leaders dedicated to increasing the efficiency of energy use. Conducts research and educational programs, and offers publications for use by the public.

American Paper Institute
260 Madison Ave.
New York, NY 10016
(212) 340-0600

Provides information on how to recycle paper in homes, offices, and communities.

Center for Environmental Education
1725 DeSales St., NW, #500
Washington, DC 20036
(202) 429-5609

Provides information services about environmental issues and problems.

Citizen's Clearinghouse for Hazardous Waste
PO Box 926
Arlington, VA 22216
(703) 276-7070

A nonprofit environmental crisis center. Collects data from grassroots environmental groups around the country, runs the Grassroots Movement Campaign which works for waste reduction and recycling, and protests toxic waste.

Conservation and Renewable Energy Inquiry and Referral Service (CAREIRS)
Box 8900
Silver Spring, MD 20907
(800) 523-2929
Provides basic information on energy conservation and renewable types of energy such as solar, wind, hydroelectric, photovoltaic, geothermal, and bioconversion.

Environmental Action Foundation
1525 New Hampshire Ave., NW
Washington, DC 20036
(202) 745-4870
Provides alternatives to inefficient waste management by promoting decreased production of wastes, reuse, recycling, and composting.

Environmental Defense Fund
257 Park Ave. South
New York, NY 10010
(212) 505-2100/(800) CALL-EDF
Sponsors a national recycling campaign and publishes a brochure on recycling.

National Recycling Coalition
110 30th St.
Suite 305
Washington, DC 20007
(202) 625-6406
Represents and provides information about individual recycling companies and local recycling groups around the country.

National Solid Wastes Management Association
1730 Rhode Island Ave.
Suite 1000
Washington, DC 20036
(202) 659-4613
Represents privately owned waste industries; provides data and statistics about landfills, incineration, and other garbage-related operations; and promotes solutions to modern refuse problems.

Plastics Recycling Foundation (PRF)
1275 K St., NW
Suite 400
Washington, DC 20005
(202) 371-5200

Sponsors research on plastics recycling.

U.S. Environmental Protection Agency (EPA)
401 M St., NW
Washington, DC 20460
(202) 260-2090

Protects and enhances the environment; controls and reduces pollution of air and water; and regulates solid waste disposal and use of pesticides, radiation, and toxic substances.

U.S. Public Interest Group
215 Pennsylvania Ave., SE
Washington, DC 20003
(202) 546-9707

Provides information on the refuse-disposal problem and promotes various recycling programs.

Worldwatch Institute
1776 Massachusetts Ave., NW
Washington, DC 20036
(202) 452-1999

Publishes the bimonthly magazine *World Watch*, which provides information on environmental issues including recycling; also publishes "Materials Recycling: The Virtue of Necessity," (Worldwatch Paper #56), a copy of which is available upon request.

Suggestions for Further Reading

Gary D. Branson, *A Complete Guide to Recycling at Home.* White Hall, VA: Betterway Publications, 1991.

Lester R. Brown, ed., *The World Watch Reader on Global Environmental Issues.* New York: W.W. Norton, 1991.

Earthworks Group, *50 Simple Things Kids Can Do to Save the Earth.* Kansas City, MO: Andrews and McMeel, 1990.

Sherry Koehler, ed., *It's Your Environment: Things to Think About—Things to Do.* New York: Scribner's, 1976.

Karen O'Conner, *Garbage.* San Diego: Lucent Books, 1989.

Anne Pederson, *The Kids' Environmental Book: What's Awry and Why.* Sante Fe, NM: John Muir Publications, 1991.

Steve Sidmore, *What a Load of Trash!* Brookfield, CT: Millbrook Press, 1991.

Richard Zimmerman, *What Can I Do to Make a Difference? A Positive Action Sourcebook.* New York: Penguin Books, 1991.

Works Consulted

Phyllis Austin, "What?! There's Garbage in Japan?" *Garbage*, November/December 1991.

M.D. Brown, "Recycling and Reusing," *Current Health*, February 1991.

Editors of *Buzzworm Magazine, 1992 Earth Journal: Environmental Almanac and Resource Directory*. Boulder, CO: Buzzworm Books, 1991.

Andrew Dobson, ed., *The Green Reader: Essays Toward a Sustainable Society*. San Francisco: Mercury House, 1991.

Maura Dolan, "Disposable Articles of Faith," *Los Angeles Times*, March 12, 1991.

Diane Duffy, "Recycling Controversies," *The Conservationist*, February/March 1990.

Mark Fischetti, "Everything Old Is New Again" and "No Room at the Landfill," *Omni*, January 1992.

Tom Jackson, "Recycling Report: News You Can Use," *Better Homes and Gardens*, May 1991.

Katie Kelly, *Garbage: The History and Future of Garbage in America*. New York: Saturday Review Press, 1973.

Charles H. Lipsett, *A Hundred Years of Recycling History: From Yankee Tincart Peddlers to Wall Street Scrap Giants*. New York: Atlas Publishing, 1974.

Lori Moody, "Film Studios Put Focus on Recycling," *The San Diego Union*, October 6, 1991.

P. Nutly, "Recycling Becomes Big Business," *Fortune*, August 13, 1990.

Michael G. Renner, "Saving the Earth, Creating Jobs," *World Watch*, January/February 1992.

L. Savage, "Recycling: A Primer on Treating Trash as a Resource," *Country Journal*, January/February 1990.

Lynn Scarlett, "Will Recycling Help the Environment?" *Consumer's Research Magazine*, March 1991.

Alan Ternes, "The Endless Cycle," *Natural History*, May 1990.

John E. Young, "Aluminum's Real Tab," *World Watch*, March/April 1992.

John E. Young, "Tossing the Throwaway Habit," *World Watch*, May/June 1991.

Richard Zimmerman, *What Can I Do to Make a Difference? A Positive Action Sourcebook*. New York: Penguin Books, 1991.

Index

ALCOA, 28
aluminum
  amount recycled, 26
American Paper Institute, 56, 85
Amoco Chemical Company
  recycling efforts of, 7, 76
AT&T
  recycling efforts of, 23

batteries
  disposal of, 56-58
  recycling of, 36
    economics of, 56-57
Battery Council International, 57-58
biodegradable bags
  as no substitute for recycling, 61-63
  drawbacks to, 59-61
Blakey, Allen, 15, 55
Boy Scouts
  recycling efforts of, 23
Branson, Gary, 10
businesses
  recycling efforts of, 70-71

California Environmental Media
  Association, 73
California
  recycling law, 27
Canada
  garbage problem in, 13
Center for the Biology of Natural
  Systems (CBNS)
  recycling study, 67
Chicago
  landfill problems of, 15
communities
  recycling efforts of, 65-70
    examples of, 80-85
Constitution
  hull made from recycled metal, 19

deposits, on bottles, 28
diapers
  cloth versus disposable, 39-42
  disposable

amount produced each year, 40
Dow Chemical Company, 61
Duffy, Diane, 47, 56, 63

Earth Day, 21-22, 23
entertainment industry
  recycling efforts in, 72-75
environment
  impact of recycling on, 31-47
  recycling as a way to help, 9
Environmental Defense Fund, 71
Environmental Protection Agency
  (EPA)
  estimate of number of landfills,
    14-15
  regulations regarding battery
    disposal, 59
  statistics on number of batteries
    recycled, 58
  statistics on recycling increase, 27

Ferretti, Will, 53
foam
  recycling of, 8

garbage
  amount produced in United States,
    9-10
  amount produced worldwide,
    10-11
  crisis
    causes of, 13-14
  pickup
    increasing costs to encourage
      recycling, 67-70
Girl Scouts
  recycling efforts of, 23
glass bottles
  recycling of, 8
Goodyear Rubber Company, 75
grassroots recycling programs, 27
Green Movement
  rise of, 24

hazardous waste

amount of generated by consumers,
  35-36
High Bridge, New Jersey
  recycling program of, 69-70
Hiroshima
  garbage problem in, 13
home recycling efforts, 20-21

incinerators
  recycling reduces need for, 36-37,
  38
industry
  as creator of garbage, 13

Japan
  amount of garbage produced by,
  12-13
  amount of money spent on
  incinerators, 38-39
  highest amount of aluminum
  recycled, 26

Kamena, Karl, 61
Kelly, Katie, 51, 76
Kraner, Thomas, 56

landfills
  as recycling centers, 28
  drawbacks of, 14-15
  hazardous wastes in, 36
  recycling, 76-79
  recycling's impact on, 34-35
Lipsett, Charles, 17, 18, 20
logging
  environmental damage caused by,
  33-34
Los Angeles
  landfill problems of, 15
lumber
  made from recycled polystyrene, 76

McDonald's Company
  recycling efforts of, 70-72
McRecycle USA, 71-72
Massachusetts
  historical recycling efforts of, 17
metal
  amount recycled worldwide, 26
  mining of, 32
Mighdoll, M.J., 22-23
Mount Trashmore, 78-79

National Association of Secondary
  Material Industries, 23, 24
National Solid Wastes Management

Association, 15, 55
natural resources
  recycling conserves, 31-32
New England
  early recycling efforts of, 19
newspapers
  recycling
    amount needed to save a tree,
    32-33
    economics of, 51-56
    increase in led to market glut,
    54-55
    process of, 8-9
New York City
  recycling law, 27
New York Times
  amount of paper needed to produce,
  32
Nielsen, Paul, 49, 50
Nosenchuck, Norman H., 62

oil
  recycling conserves, 32
  spills, 9

packaging
  amount of
    as harmful, 42-43
    benefits to, 44
    recycling of, 10
paper
  amount used annually, 32
  drive
    how to conduct, 83-85
  manufacturers
    new products of, 24
    role in recycling newspapers, 52
  recycling of
    kind of quality needed, 53
    reduces need for logging, 33
    reduces pollution, 34
Paramount Studios
  recycling efforts of, 74
plastic
  use of in building materials, 75-76
  recycling of, 9
    difficulties in, 49-50
Pollock-Shea, Cynthia, 39
pollution
  amount of caused by incinerators,
  36-37, 38
  recycling reduces, 31, 34
polystyrene
  amount produced by McDonald's,
  71-72

recycling of, 76
  difficulty in, 43
population
  amount of garbage generated by,
    10
Porter, Abel, 18-19
precycling
  definition of, 80
  examples of, 80-81
Proctor & Gamble, 41-42

Rancourt, Arlene and Roger, 7
recycling
  amount of increase in, 25-26
  as big business, 27-28
  as way to reduce landfills, 34-35
  complications of, 39-40
  definition of, 7-8
  grassroots programs, 27
  history of, 17-18
  how to, 82-83
  profit motive prevents increase in,
    50-51
  programs
    examples of, 80-85
  requires effort, 62
Redford, Lola, 23
Revere, Paul, 19
Riverview, Michigan
  efforts at recycling landfills, 77-79

Safe Sets, 73-74
Satt, Joan, 74
Scarlett, Lynn, 43-44, 68
scrap metal
  recycling of, 18-19
  during WWII, 20
Seattle, Washington
  recycling program of, 67-69
Spahn, Andy, 73
state laws
  on banning certain packaging
    materials, 43
  on recycling, 27

Tallen, Kathy, 7
television shows
  depicting recycling in, 72-73
Thomas, Tony, 73
tires
  recycling of, 75
trees
  recycling as a way to conserve, 32
trucks
  increase in number due to

recycling, 44-45

United States
  amount of garbage produced by,
    9-12
  amount of money spent on
    incinerators, 38-39
United States Congress
  hearings on recycling, 23-24
U.S. Bureau of Mines, 75-76

Warner Brothers,
  recycling efforts of, 74
wars
  need for recycling during, 19-20
Western Europe
  amount of aluminum recycled, 26
wood recycling, 73-74
World Resources Institute, 39
World War II
  scrap metal drive during, 20
Worldwatch Institute, 38

Young, John E., 12, 36-37, 38

Zimmerman, Richard, 29, 82, 83

About the Author

Don Nardo is an actor, film director, and composer, as well as an award-winning writer. As an actor, he has appeared in more than fifty stage productions. He has also worked before or behind the camera in twenty films. Several of his musical compositions, including a young person's version of *The War of the Worlds* and the oratorio *Richard III*, have been played by regional orchestras. Mr. Nardo's writing credits include short stories, articles, and more than thirty-five books, including *Lasers*, *Anxiety and Phobias*, *Gravity*, *Germs*, *Eating Disorders*, *Charles Darwin*, and *The War of 1812*. Among his other writings are an episode of ABC's "Spenser: For Hire" and numerous screenplays. Mr. Nardo lives with his wife, Christine, on Cape Cod, Massachusetts.

Picture Credits